Why Things Don't Work
PLANE

Published by Raintree, a division of Reed Elsevier, Inc.
Chicago, Illinois

Customer Service 888-363-4266
Visit our website at www.raintreelibrary.com

Why Things Don't Work PLANE
was produced by

David West 👫 **Children's Books**
7 Princeton Court
55 Felsham Road
London SW15 1AZ

Editor: Dominique Crowley
Consultant: Nigel Parker

11 10 09 08 07
10 9 8 7 6 5 4 3 2 1

Library of Congress Cataloging-in-Publication Data

West, David.
  Why things don't work. Plane / David West.
    p. cm. -- (Why things don't work)
  Includes index.
  ISBN 1-4109-2556-0
  1. Airplanes--Maintenance and repair--Juvenile literature. 2.
Airplanes--Parts--Juvenile literature. I. Title. II. Title: Plane. III.
Series: West, David. Why things don't work.
  TL671.9.W47 2006
  629.134'6--dc22
                                                    2006017943

Printed and bound in China

Why Things Don't Work

PLANE

by David West

Raintree
Chicago, Illinois

Contents

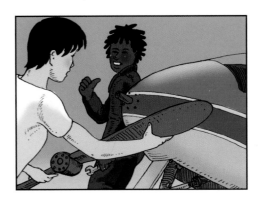

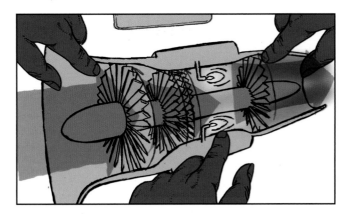

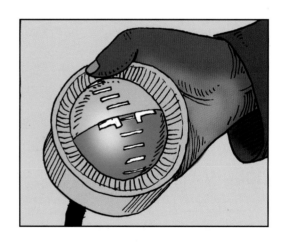

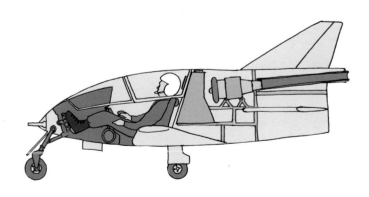

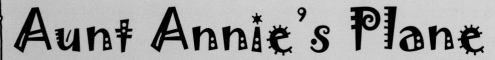

Aunt Annie's Plane

ALICE HAS JUST PASSED HER FLYING TEST AND WANTS TO FLY HER AUNT'S PLANE. UNFORTUNATELY, IT DOESN'T WORK. IT HASN'T BEEN FLOWN FOR YEARS AND THERE ARE PARTS OF THE PLANE SCATTERED AROUND.

ALSO, THERE ARE SOME OTHER PROBLEMS...

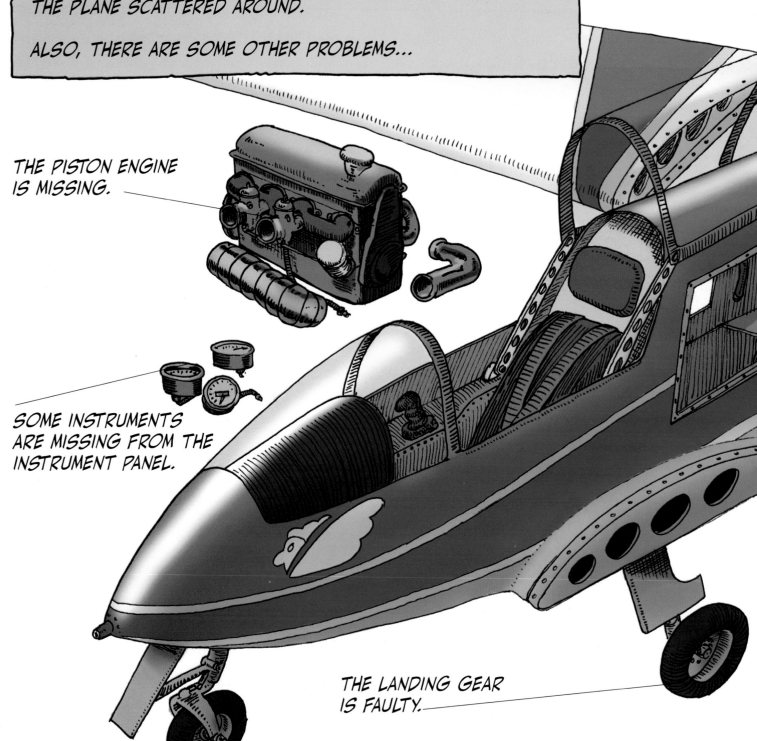

THE PISTON ENGINE IS MISSING.

SOME INSTRUMENTS ARE MISSING FROM THE INSTRUMENT PANEL.

THE LANDING GEAR IS FAULTY.

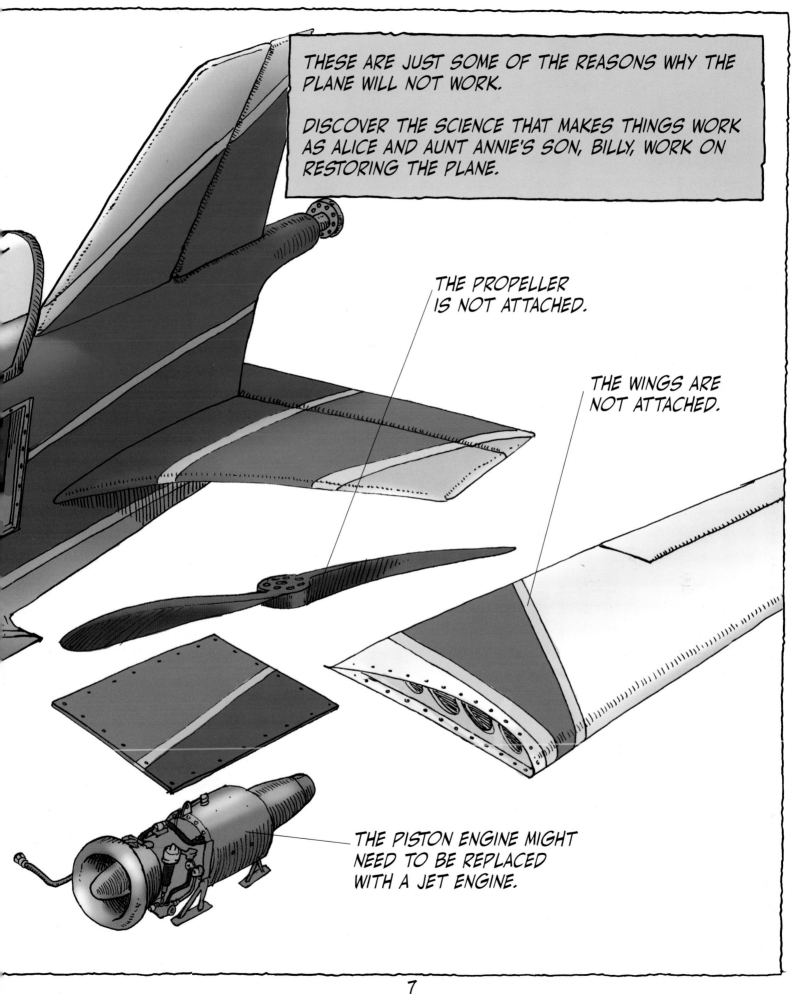

THESE ARE JUST SOME OF THE REASONS WHY THE PLANE WILL NOT WORK.

DISCOVER THE SCIENCE THAT MAKES THINGS WORK AS ALICE AND AUNT ANNIE'S SON, BILLY, WORK ON RESTORING THE PLANE.

THE PROPELLER IS NOT ATTACHED.

THE WINGS ARE NOT ATTACHED.

THE PISTON ENGINE MIGHT NEED TO BE REPLACED WITH A JET ENGINE.

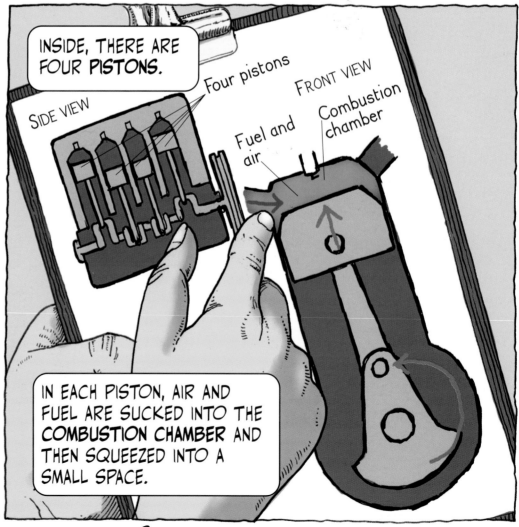

LET'S SEE IF IT WILL TURN THE PROPELLER.

WHERE'S THE PROPELLER?

OH. THERE IT IS, ON THE GROUND.

LET'S SEE. NOW, WHERE DOES IT GO?

IT GOES AT THE BACK.

AT THE BACK?

YES. THEY CAN PUSH PLANES FROM BEHIND, AS WELL AS PULL THEM FROM THE FRONT.

THE BLADES ON A PROPELLER ARE SHAPED LIKE THIS.

WHEN THEY SPIN, THE AIR RUSHING OVER THE FRONT SURFACE HAS FURTHER TO TRAVEL. THIS CREATES A **LOW AIR PRESSURE** AREA IN FRONT.

Red areas show the propeller **cross section**

Rotation of propeller

Air flow

Low air pressure

Direction of plane

Thrust

THE PROPELLER MOVES INTO THE LOW PRESSURE AREA AND SO MOVES FORWARD, PROVIDING A BACKWARD **THRUST.**

IT MOVES THROUGH THE AIR LIKE A SCREW. THIS IS WHY PROPELLERS ARE SOMETIMES CALLED AIRSCREWS.

YOU CAN PUT THE PROPELLER AT THE FRONT OR AT THE BACK. IT STILL MOVES THE PLANE IN THE SAME DIRECTION.

Thrust

Direction

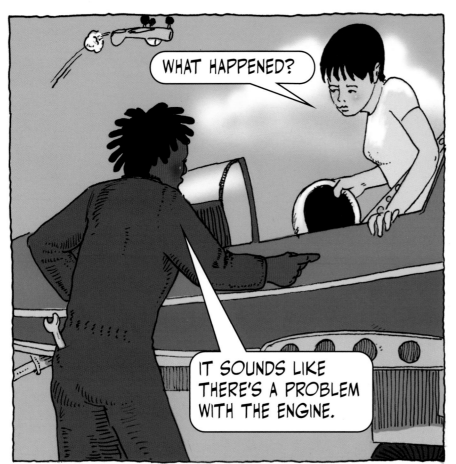

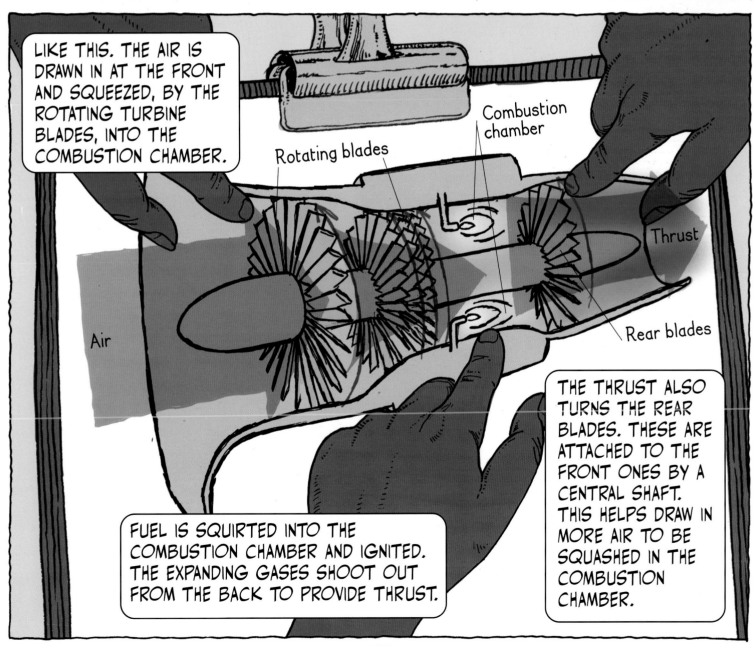

16

SOON, WE HAD THE JET ENGINE IN PLACE.

JET ENGINES USE A DIFFERENT FUEL FROM PISTON ENGINES. SO WE HAD BETTER CHANGE THE FUEL.

LET'S SEE IF THE ENGINE WORKS.

WEEEEEEEEEEEE

NICE.

WINGS WORK LIKE THIS.

AIR RUSHING OVER THE TOP HAS FURTHER TO GO AND SO TRAVELS FASTER THAN THE AIR UNDERNEATH.

LIFT

Low air pressure area

Faster traveling air

Slower traveling air

Direction of wing

THE FASTER AIR CREATES AN AREA OF LOW AIR PRESSURE, SO THE WING MOVES UP INTO THIS AREA. THIS IS CALLED LIFT.

LOOK, I'LL SHOW YOU WITH THIS PIECE OF PAPER.

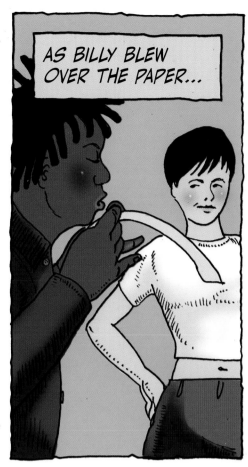

AS BILLY BLEW OVER THE PAPER...

...IT ROSE UPWARD.

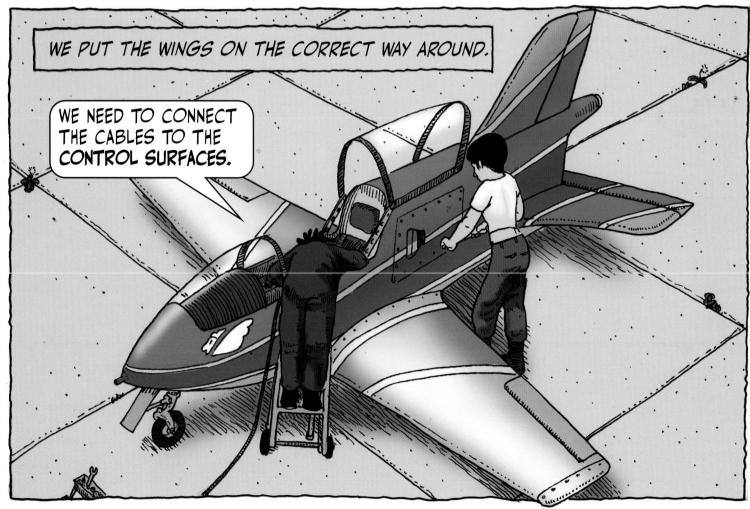

WE PUT THE WINGS ON THE CORRECT WAY AROUND.

WE NEED TO CONNECT THE CABLES TO THE CONTROL SURFACES.

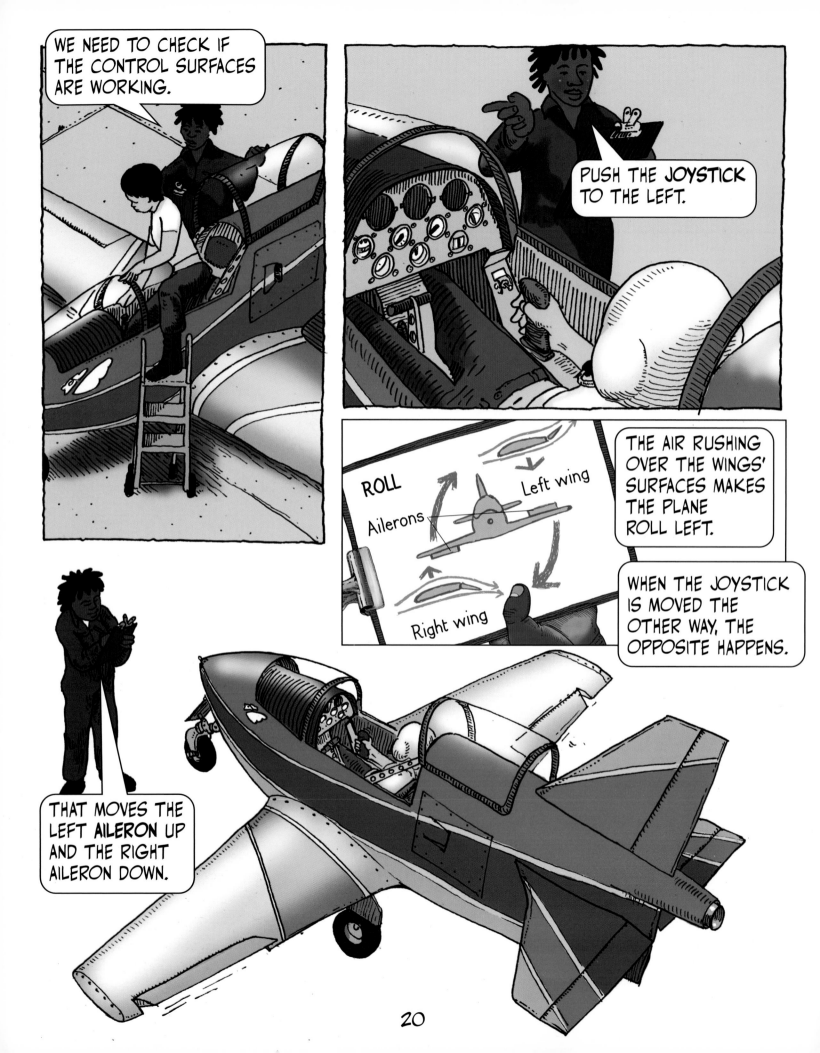

WE NEED TO CHECK IF THE CONTROL SURFACES ARE WORKING.

PUSH THE **JOYSTICK** TO THE LEFT.

ROLL

Ailerons

Left wing

Right wing

THE AIR RUSHING OVER THE WINGS' SURFACES MAKES THE PLANE ROLL LEFT.

WHEN THE JOYSTICK IS MOVED THE OTHER WAY, THE OPPOSITE HAPPENS.

THAT MOVES THE LEFT **AILERON** UP AND THE RIGHT AILERON DOWN.

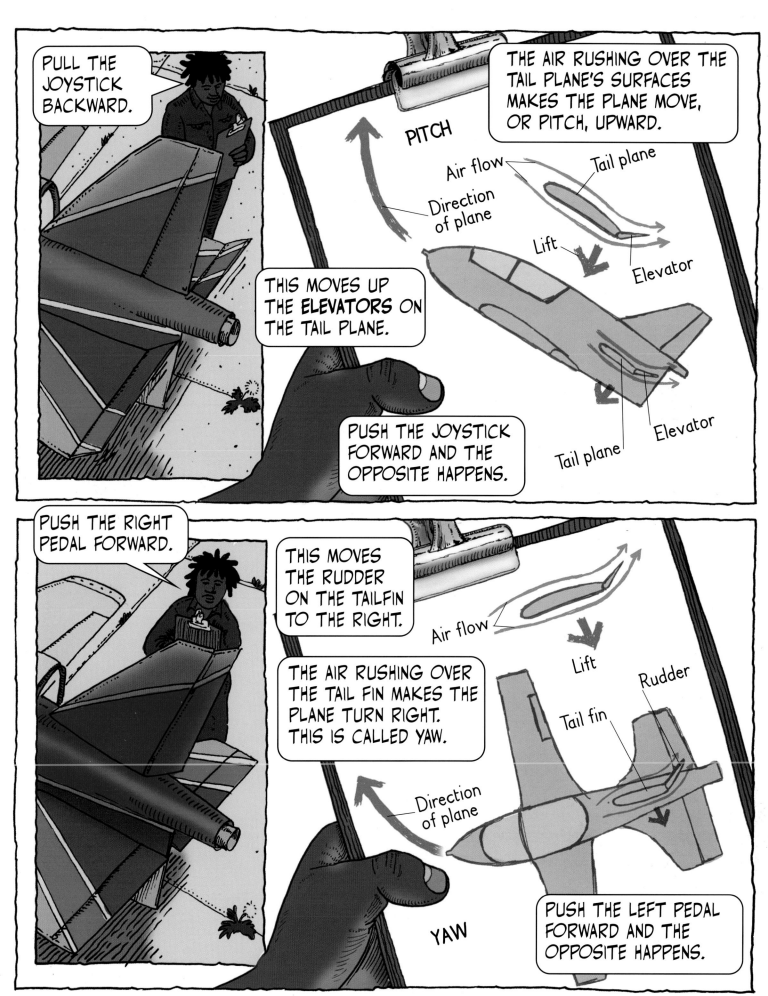

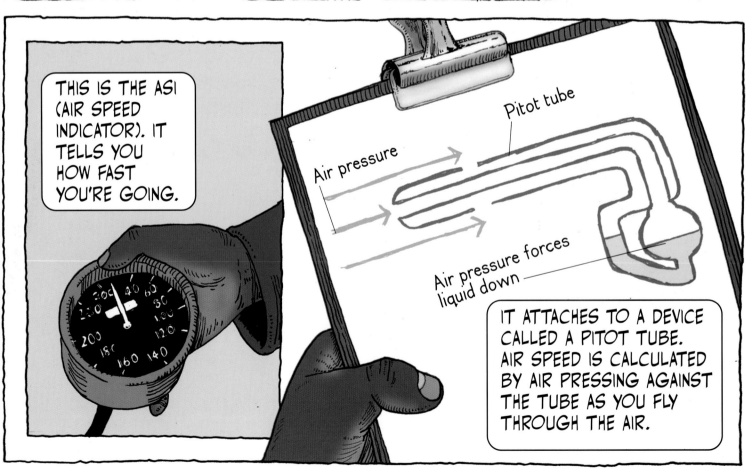

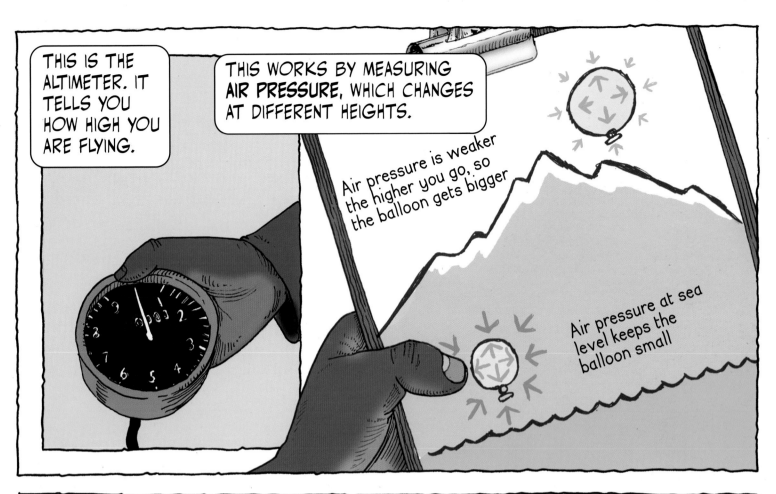

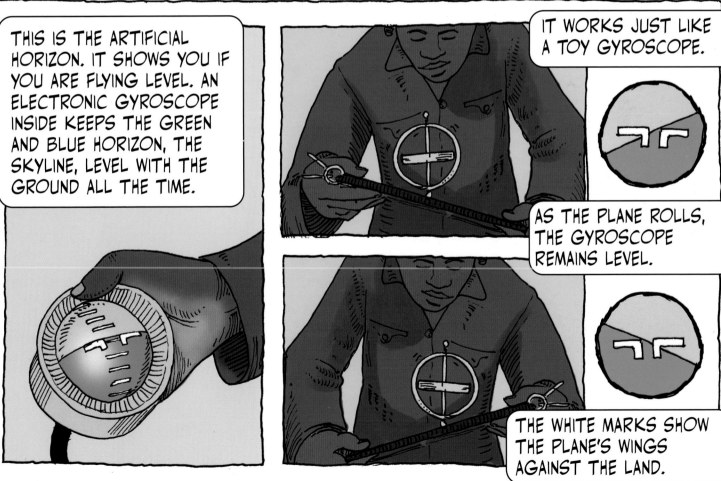

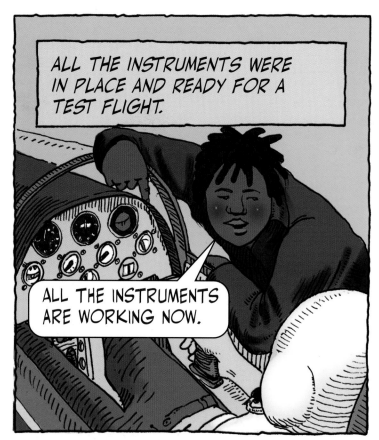

ALL THE INSTRUMENTS WERE IN PLACE AND READY FOR A TEST FLIGHT.

ALL THE INSTRUMENTS ARE WORKING NOW.

BILLY WENT INTO THE CONTROL TOWER TO CHECK FOR OTHER AIR TRAFFIC.

ALICE, YOU CAN TAXI OUT TO THE RUNWAY.

ROGER THAT, BILLY.

YOU ARE CLEAR FOR TAKE OFF.

ROGER THAT, BILLY.

WHOOOOOOOSH

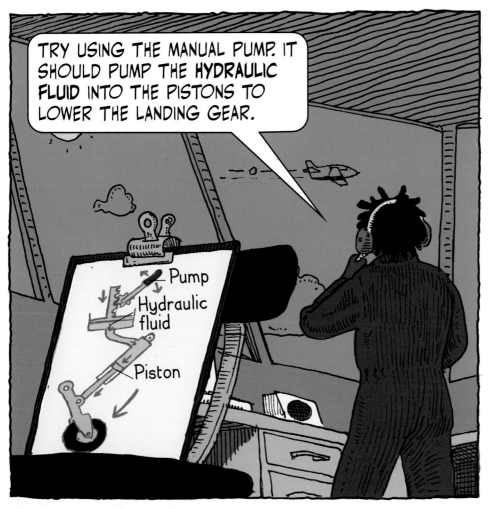

THE FOLLOWING WEEK, WE SET OFF FOR AN AIR SHOW.

WE SAW A COPY OF THE WRIGHT FLYER.

THIS WAS THE FIRST PLANE TO FLY. IT WAS MADE AND FLOWN BY THE WRIGHT BROTHERS IN 1904.

THERE WERE ALSO SOME AMAZING PLANES FROM WORLD WAR II.

LOOK IT'S A FLYING FORTRESS BOMBER.

AND A MUSTANG FIGHTER.

THEN, SOME AWESOME STEALTH FIGHTERS FLEW BY.

WE ALSO SAW THE WORLD'S BIGGEST MODEL PLANE.

IT'S AN AIRBUS SUPERJUMBO. THE JET ENGINES ARE REAL MINIATURE JET ENGINES!

THEN IT WAS MY TURN...

...AND HERE COMES ALICE IN A BD-5, THE THE WORLD'S SMALLEST JET PLANE.

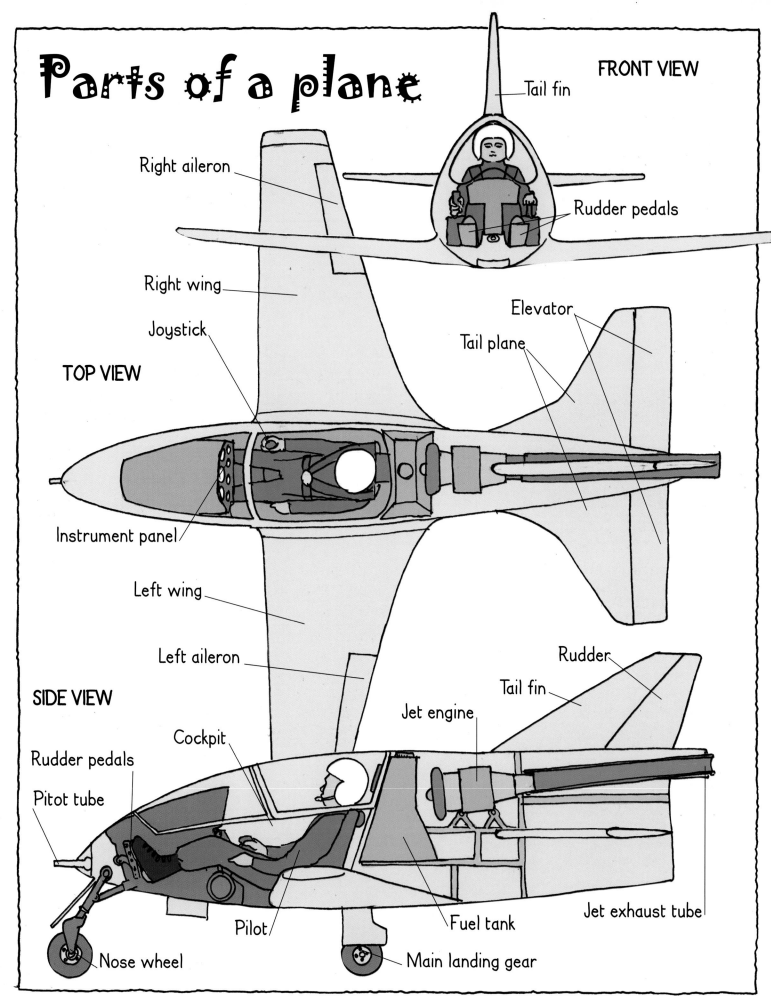

Parts of a plane

Tail fin

Right aileron

Rudder pedals

Right wing

Elevator

Tail plane

TOP VIEW

Joystick

Instrument panel

Left wing

Left aileron

Rudder

Tail fin

Jet engine

SIDE VIEW

Rudder pedals

Cockpit

Pitot tube

Pilot

Fuel tank

Jet exhaust tube

Nose wheel

Main landing gear

30

Glossary

AILERONS
MOVABLE FLAPS ON THE WINGS THAT MAKE THE PLANE ROLL

AIR PRESSURE
THE FORCE OF AIR CREATED BY THE AMOUNT OR MOVEMENT OF AIR

COMBUSTION CHAMBER
THE AREA OF AN ENGINE WHERE THE FUEL/AIR MIXTURE IS SET ON FIRE

CONTROL SURFACES
THE MOVABLE PARTS ON THE WINGS AND TAIL OF A PLANE THAT CONTROL THE WAY THE PLANE MOVES IN THE AIR

CRANKSHAFT
THE ROTATING SHAFT AT THE BOTTOM OF THE ENGINE THAT IS TURNED BY THE PISTONS

CROSS SECTION
THE SHAPE OF AN OBJECT WHEN IT IS SLICED THROUGH BY AN IMAGINARY BLADE

ELEVATORS
MOVABLE FLAPS ON THE TAIL PLANE THAT MAKE THE PLANE PITCH UP OR DOWN

HYDRAULIC FLUID
SPECIAL LIQUID USED TO MOVE PISTONS

IGNITE
TO SET ON FIRE

JOYSTICK
THE HAND-OPERATED CONTROL COLUMN THAT CONTROLS THE ROLL AND PITCH OF THE PLANE

LANDING GEAR
WHEELS AND SUPPORTING PARTS OF A PLANE THAT ALLOW IT TO TAKE OFF AND LAND

LOW AIR PRESSURE AREA
AN AREA OF AIR THAT HAS LESS AIR THAN ITS SURROUNDING AREA. IF THE PRESSURE IS LOW ENOUGH IT WILL DRAW IN OBJECTS OR AIR TO EQUALIZE THE PRESSURE.

PISTON
A METAL CYLINDER THAT MOVES BACK AND FORTH INSIDE ANOTHER CYLINDER

PROPSHAFT (PROPELLER SHAFT)
A REVOLVING ROD THAT CONNECTS THE ENGINE TO THE PROPELLER

RUDDER
MOVABLE FLAP ON THE TAIL FIN THAT MAKES THE PLANE YAW LEFT OR RIGHT

SPARK PLUG
A DEVICE THAT CAUSES A SPARK TO BE CREATED

THRUST
A STRONG, CONTINUOUS FORCE OF PRESSURE

Index